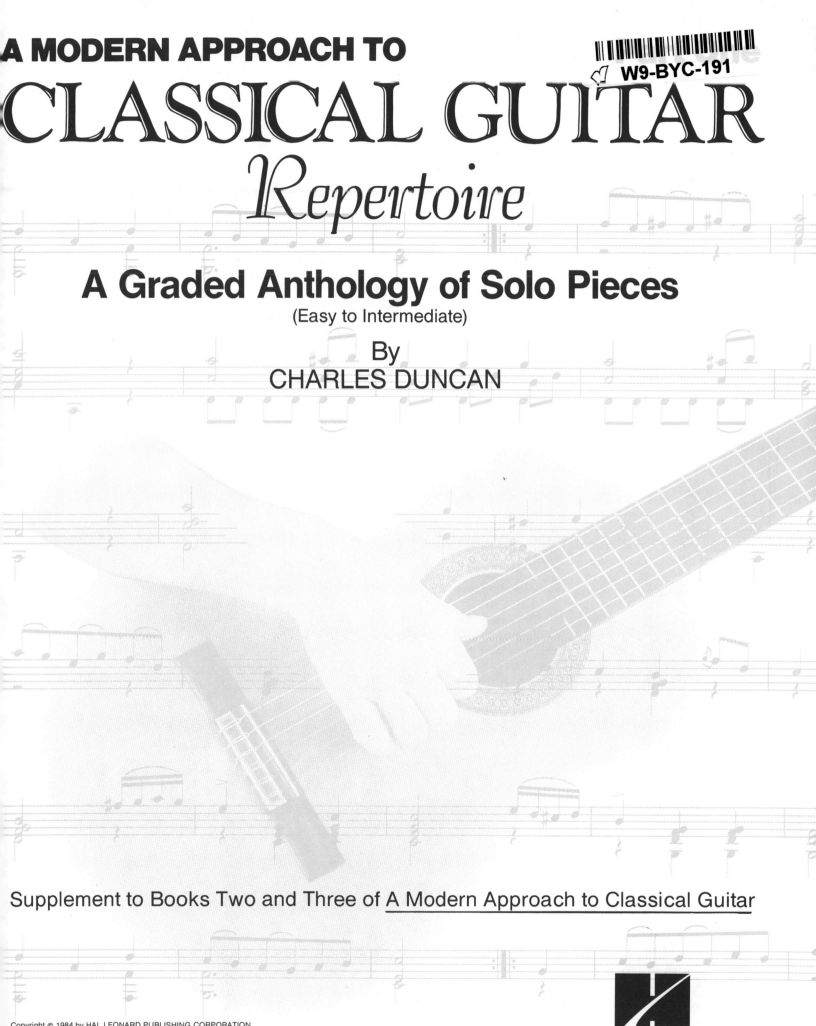

A MODERN APPROACH TO
CLASSICAL GUITAR
Repertoire

A Graded Anthology of Solo Pieces
(Easy to Intermediate)

By
CHARLES DUNCAN

Supplement to Books Two and Three of A Modern Approach to Classical Guitar

HAL•LEONARD®
7777 W. BLUEMOUND RD. P.O. BOX 13819
MILWAUKEE, WISCONSIN 53213

Charles Duncan

ABOUT THE AUTHOR

Charles Duncan is the author of Hal Leonard's **A MODERN APPROACH TO CLASSICAL GUITAR** Books One, Two, Three-and **FINGERSTYLE POP CLASSICS.**

With an extensive background of international guitar study (including a scholarship to the Segovia Master Class in Santiago de Compostela, Spain), Charles Duncan is rapidly emerging as one of the most influential teacher-performers of the classical guitar today. He is the author of numerous articles on guitar technique and a major book, *THE ART OF CLASSICAL GUITAR PLAYING* (Summy-Birchard), which is widely used as an advanced-level text in colleges and conservatories. His performances throughout the eastern United States and Canada have been received with warm audience response and critical acclaim. Charles Duncan has a broad-ranging command of the instrument that includes flamenco and jazz in addition to traditional classical guitar repertoire. An outstanding ensemble player, he has made a highly-acclaimed recording, *FOUR CENTURIES OF MUSIC FOR FLUTE AND GUITAR* (Golden Crest). He currently serves on the music faculty of Emory University, is a former president of the Atlanta Music Teachers' Association, and writes the "Guitar Forum" column for AMERICAN STRING TEACHER.

FOREWORD

A Modern Approach to Classical Guitar Repertoire represents a graded anthology of some of the most attractive music from the standard repertoire of 16th through 19th century pieces. The music is carefully arranged in sequence according to the level of difficulty. Part 1 progresses from easy to intermediate level pieces; Part 2 from intermediate through moderately difficult.

These books are also cross-indexed by specific achievement level with Books 2 and 3 of **A Modern Approach To Classical Guitar Playing.** (See CONTENTS.) As such, they may be used as supplements to the method for additional study or recreation.

CONTENTS

ALPHABETICAL LIST OF COMPOSERS

ALLEGRETTO

Fernando Sor

*Place LH fingers simultaneously for a C chord, i.e.

SCOTTISH DANCE

Mauro Giuliani

*Place LH fingers simultaneously for an Am chord, i.e.

MODERATO

Fernando Sor

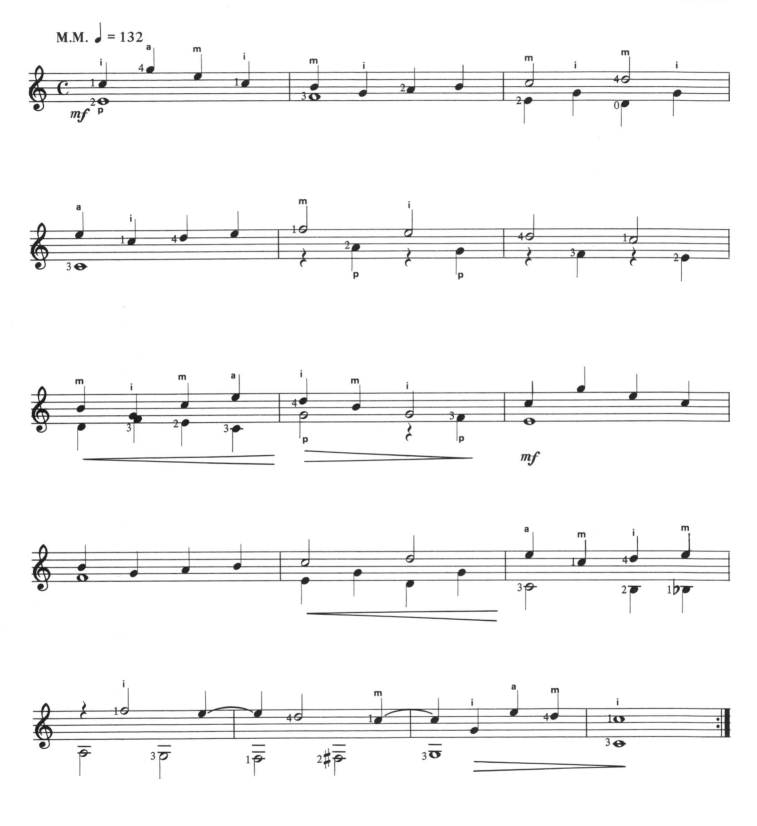

ALLEGRETTO

Fernando Sor

ALLEGRO

Mauro Giuliani

WALTZ IN G

Ferdinand Carulli

*In $\frac{3}{8}$ time, the eighth note receives one beat. Count each measure 1-2-3, 1-2-3, etc. in this piece.

ANDANTINO

Fernando Sor

ENGLISH DANCE

Ferdinand Carulli

ANDANTE

Matteo Carcassi

M.M. ♩ = 84

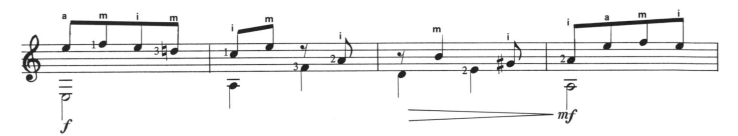

ANDANTE GRAZIOSO

Ferdinand Carulli

2d time rit.

ANDANTE

Fernando Sor

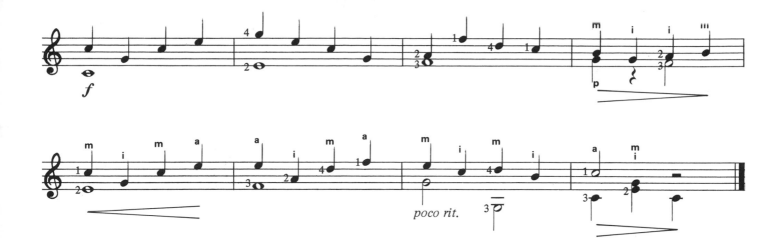

MINUET

Johann Krieger

ANDANTINO

Mauro Giuliani

poco rit.

ANDANTINO

Matteo Carcassi

M.M. ♩ = 52

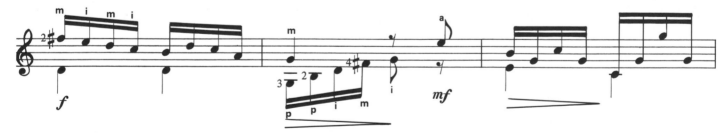

2d time rit.

SICILIANA

Ferdinand Carulli

Larghetto M.M. ♪. = 48

CASTELLANA

Fabritio Caroso

*Half-bar (2 strings) at the first fret.

ANDANTINO

Ferdinand Carulli

M.M. ♩. = 52

GREENSLEEVES

Anonymous
(16th Century)

Largo M.M. ♩. = 44

poco rit.

ANDANTE

M.M. ♩ = 63

Fernando Sor

ALLEGRETTO

Ferdinand Carulli

ETUDE

Ferdinand Carulli

MINUET

Robert de Visée

ANDANTE

Ferdinand Carulli

ETUDE IN Am

Matteo Carcassi

THE REAPERS

François Couperín

MINUET

Georg Philipp Telemann

Allegretto M.M. ♩ = 112

*Half-bar (3 strings) at the second fret.

WALTZ

Ferdinand Carulli

Allegro M.M. ♪ = 126

*Play the bass and treble notes simultaneously. Their separation, here and in many similar cases, is merely a typographical necessity.

AIR

Anonymous
(16th Century)

ANDANTE

Fernando Sor

*A double-dot increases a note-value by half again, or a total of three-fourths. Thus, the double-dotted quarter note/sixteenth figure here and in measure 14 equals ♩ ♪. ♪ ♩.

**A "hinge-bar" is used here. Keep the tip of the finger on the low B while making the bar.

ETUDE IN C

Mauro Giuliani

ALLEGRETTO

Fernando Sor

*7th fret B.

PAVANE

Anonymous
(16th Century)

Adagio M.M. ♩ = 80

*Technically the slur is from the 4th string E but is written from the G to reflect voice-leading. The E sustains by
picking up a sympathetic harmonic from the 6th string.

LARGHETTO

Fernando Sor

M.M. ♩ = 76

*or:

ALLEMANDE

Carlo Calvi

Moderato M.M. ♩ = 104

2d time rit.

*Adjust the bar to cover the 5th string.

MARCH

Fernando Sor

MODERATO

Fernando Sor

*A "crossover fingering"; keep the 3rd finger on F.

CAPRICE

Matteo Carcassi

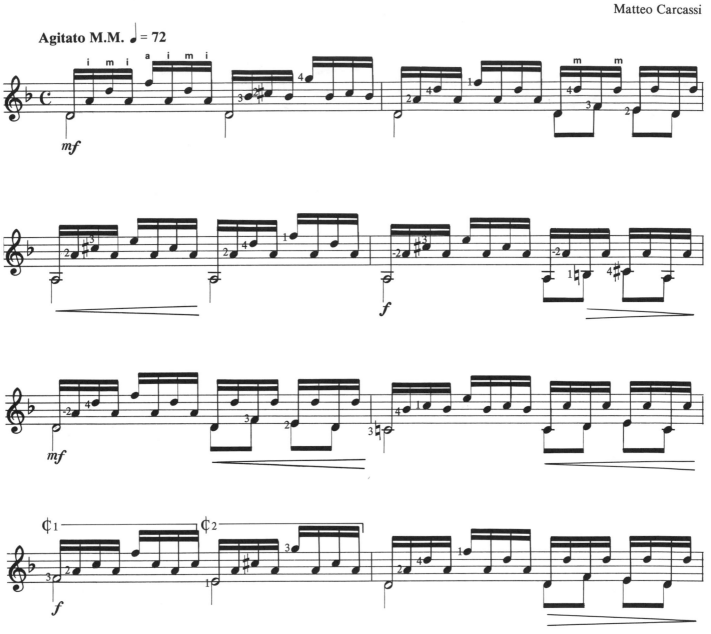

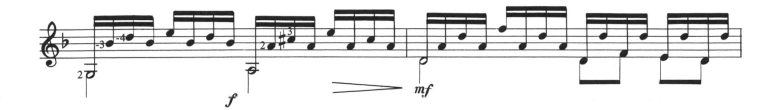

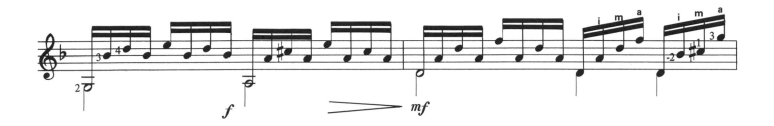

43

MINUET

Anton Diabelli

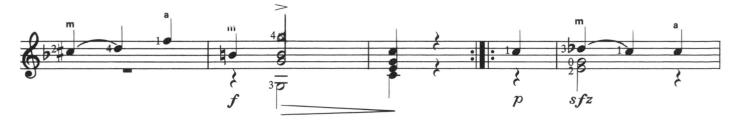

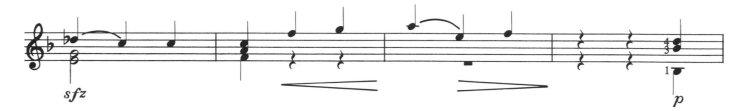

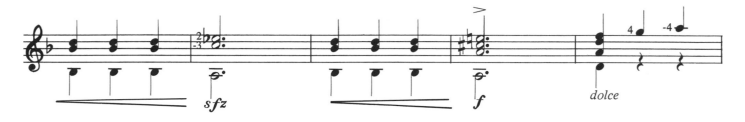

45

ARIA

Johann A. Logy

Adagio M.M. ♩ = 76

CAPRICCIO

Johann A. Logy

Allegro M.M. ♩ = 126

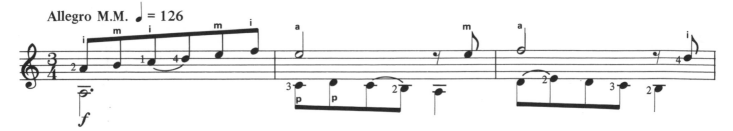

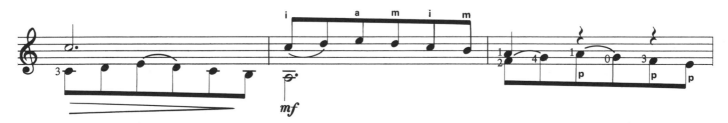

ALLEGRETTO

Fernando Sor

M.M. ♩. = 66

SARABANDE

Francesco Corbetta

50

MODERATO

M.M. ♩ = 112

Fernando Sor

AIR

Andante M.M. ♩ = 100

Henry Purcell

*Adjust the bar to a three-string bar here.

BARCAROLE

Anton Diabelli

ALLEMANDE

Anonymous
(16th Century)

Moderato M.M. ♩ = 108

1. *mf*
2. *p*

2nd time rit.

SE IO M'ACCORGO

Anonymous
(16th Century)

Larghetto M.M. ♩ = 66

DANZA

Anonymous
(16th Century)

Moderato M.M. ♩ = 116

55

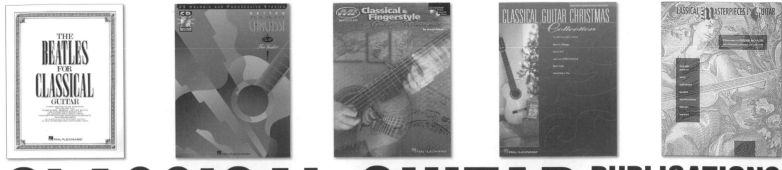

CLASSICAL GUITAR
PUBLICATIONS FROM HAL LEONARD

THE BEATLES FOR CLASSICAL GUITAR

Includes 20 solos from big Beatles hits arranged for classical guitar, complete with left-hand and right-hand fingering. Songs include: All My Loving • And I Love Her • Can't Buy Me Love • Fool on the Hill • From a Window • Hey Jude • If I Fell • Let It Be • Michelle • Norwegian Wood • Obla Di • Ticket to Ride • Yesterday • and more. Features arrangements and an introduction by Joe Washington, as well as his helpful hints on classical technique and detailed notes on how to play each song. The book also covers parts and specifications of the classical guitar, tuning, and Joe's "Strata System" – an easy-reading system applied to chord diagrams.

_____00699237 Classical Guitar $16.95

MATTEO CARCASSI – 25 MELODIC AND PROGRESSIVE STUDIES, OP. 60 • arr. Paul Henry

One of Carcassi's (1792-1853) most famous collections of classical guitar music – indispensable for the modern guitarist's musical and technical development. Performed by Paul Henry. 49-minute audio accompaniment.

00696506 Book/CD Pack $17.95

CLASSICAL & FINGERSTYLE GUITAR TECHNIQUES
INCLUDES TAB

by David Oakes • Musicians Institute

This Master Class with MI instructor David Oakes is aimed at any electric or acoustic guitarist who wants a quick, thorough grounding in the essentials of classical and fingerstyle technique. Topics covered include: arpeggios and scales, free stroke and rest stroke, P-i scale technique, three-to-a-string patterns, natural and artificial harmonics, tremolo and rasgueado, and more. The book includes 12 intensive lessons for right and left hand in standard notation & tab, and the CD features 92 solo acoustic tracks.

00695171 Book/CD Pack $14.95

CLASSICAL GUITAR CHRISTMAS COLLECTION
INCLUDES TAB

Includes classical guitar arrangements in standard notation and tablature for more than two dozen beloved carols: Angels We Have Heard on High • Auld Lang Syne • Ave Maria • Away in a Manger • Canon in D • The First Noel • God Rest Ye Merry, Gentlemen • Hark! the Herald Angels Sing • I Saw Three Ships • Jesu, Joy of Man's Desiring • Joy to the World • O Christmas Tree • O Holy Night • Silent Night • What Child Is This? • and more.

_____00699493 Guitar Solo $9.95

CLASSICAL MASTERPIECES FOR GUITAR
INCLUDES TAB

27 works by Bach, Beethoven, Handel, Mendelssohn, Mozart and more transcribed with standard notation and tablature. Now anyone can enjoy classical material regardless of their guitar background. Also features stay-open binding.

00699312 ....$12.95

FOR MORE INFORMATION, SEE YOUR LOCAL MUSIC DEALER,
OR WRITE TO:

HAL•LEONARD® CORPORATION
7777 W. BLUEMOUND RD. P.O. BOX 13819 MILWAUKEE, WI 53213
Visit Hal Leonard Online at **www.halleonard.com**

Prices, contents and availability subject to change without notice.

CLASSICAL THEMES
INCLUDES TAB

20 beloved classical themes arranged for easy guitar in large-size notes (with the note names in the note heads) and tablature. Includes: Air on the G String (Bach) • Ave Maria (Schubert) • Für Elise (Beethoven) • In the Hall of the Mountain King (Grieg) • Jesu, Joy of Man's Desiring (Bach) • Largo (Handel) • Ode to Joy (Beethoven) • Pomp and Circumstance (Elgar) • and more. Ideal for beginning or vision-impaired players.

_____00699272 E-Z Play Guitar $8.95

MASTERWORKS FOR GUITAR
INCLUDES TAB

Over 60 Favorites from Four Centuries • World's Great Classical Music

Dozens of classical masterpieces: Allemande • Bourree • Canon in D • Jesu, Joy of Man's Desiring • Lagrima • Malaguena • Mazurka • Piano Sonata No. 14 in C# (Moonlight) Op. 27 No. 2 First Movement Theme • Ode to Joy • Prelude No. I (Well-Tempered Clavier).

_____00699503 ....$16.95

A MODERN APPROACH TO CLASSICAL GUITAR • by Charles Duncan

This multi-volume method was developed to allow students to study the art of classical guitar within a new, more contemporary framework. For private, class or self-instruction. Book One incorporates chord frames and symbols, as well as a recording to assist in tuning and to provide accompaniments for at-home practice. Book One also introduces beginning fingerboard technique and music theory. Book Two and Three build upon the techniques learned in Book One.

_____00695114 Book 1 – Book Only.......................$6.95
_____00695113 Book 1 – Book/CD Pack.......................$10.95
_____00695116 Book 2 – Book Only.......................$6.95
_____00695115 Book 2 – Book/CD Pack.......................$10.95
_____00699202 Book 3 – Book Only.......................$7.95
_____00695117 Book 3 – Book/CD Pack.......................$10.95
_____00695119 Composite Book/CD Pack.......................$24.95

ANDRES SEGOVIA – 20 STUDIES FOR GUITAR • Sor/Segovia

20 studies for the classical guitar written by Beethoven's contemporary, Fernando Sor, revised, edited and fingered by the great classical guitarist Andres Segovia. These essential repertoire pieces continue to be used by teachers and students to build solid classical technique. Features a 50-minute demonstration CD.

_____00695012 Book/CD Pack.......................$17.95
_____00006363 Book Only.......................$6.95

THE FRANCISCO TÁRREGA COLLECTION
INCLUDES TAB

edited and performed by Paul Henry

Considered the father of modern classical guitar, Francisco Tárrega revolutionized guitar technique and composed a wealth of music that will be a cornerstone of classical guitar repertoire for centuries to come. This unique book/CD pack features 14 of his most outstanding pieces in standard notation and tab, edited and performed on CD by virtuoso Paul Henry. Includes: Adelita • Capricho Árabe • Estudio Brillante • Grand Jota • Lágrima • Malagueña • María • Recuerdos de la Alhambra • Tango • and more, plus bios of Tárrega and Henry.

_____00698993 Book/CD Pack $17.95

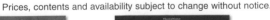

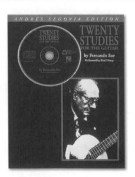

1202

СИЦИЛИАНА

Fine

D.C. al Fine

Урок 26

ПРЕЛЮДИЯ

Ф. КАРУЛЛИ (1770—1841)

Подвижно

ПРЕЛЮДИЯ 27.

А. ИВАНОВ-КРАМСКОЙ

Взволнованно

На заре ты её не буди.

Варламов

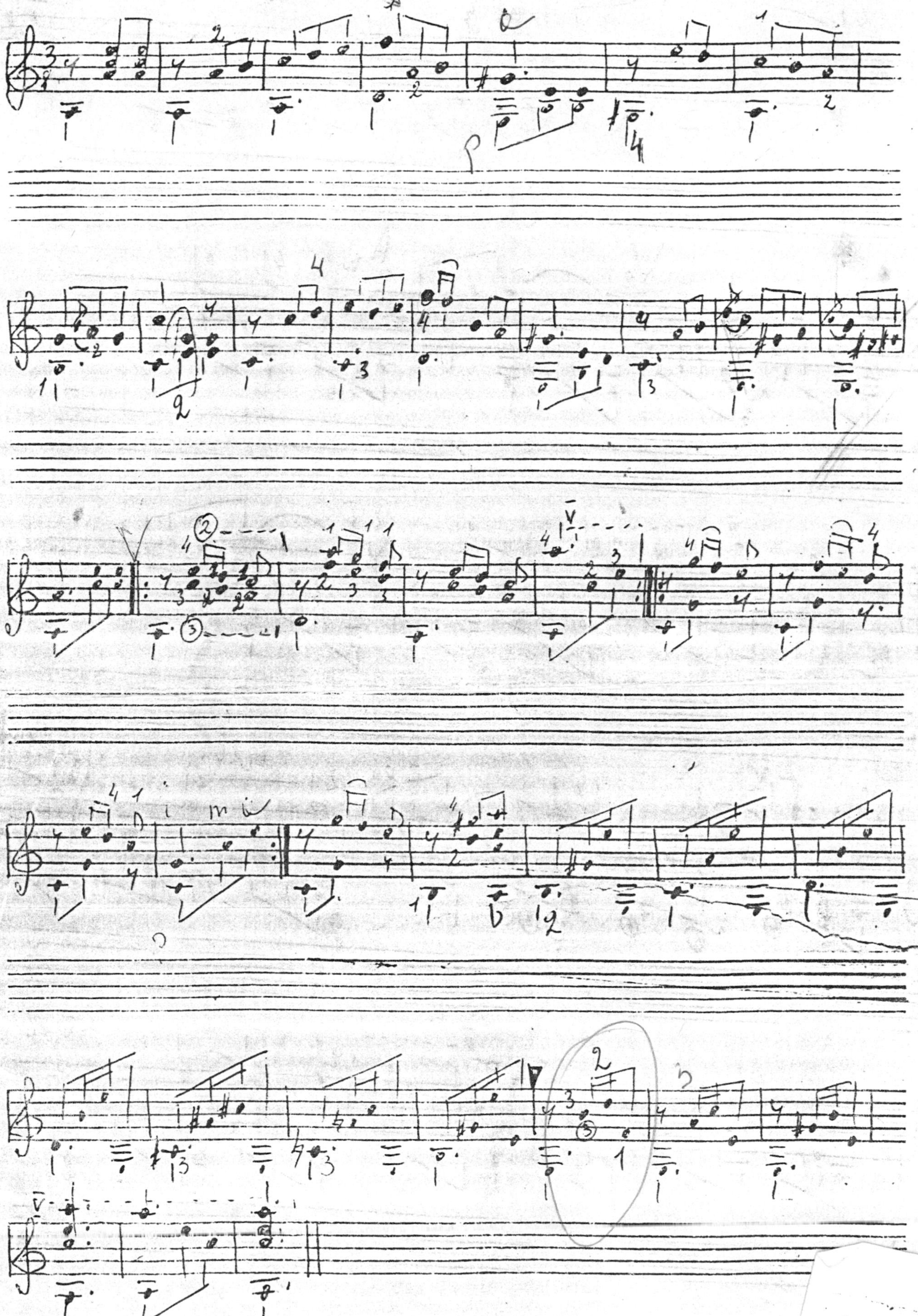

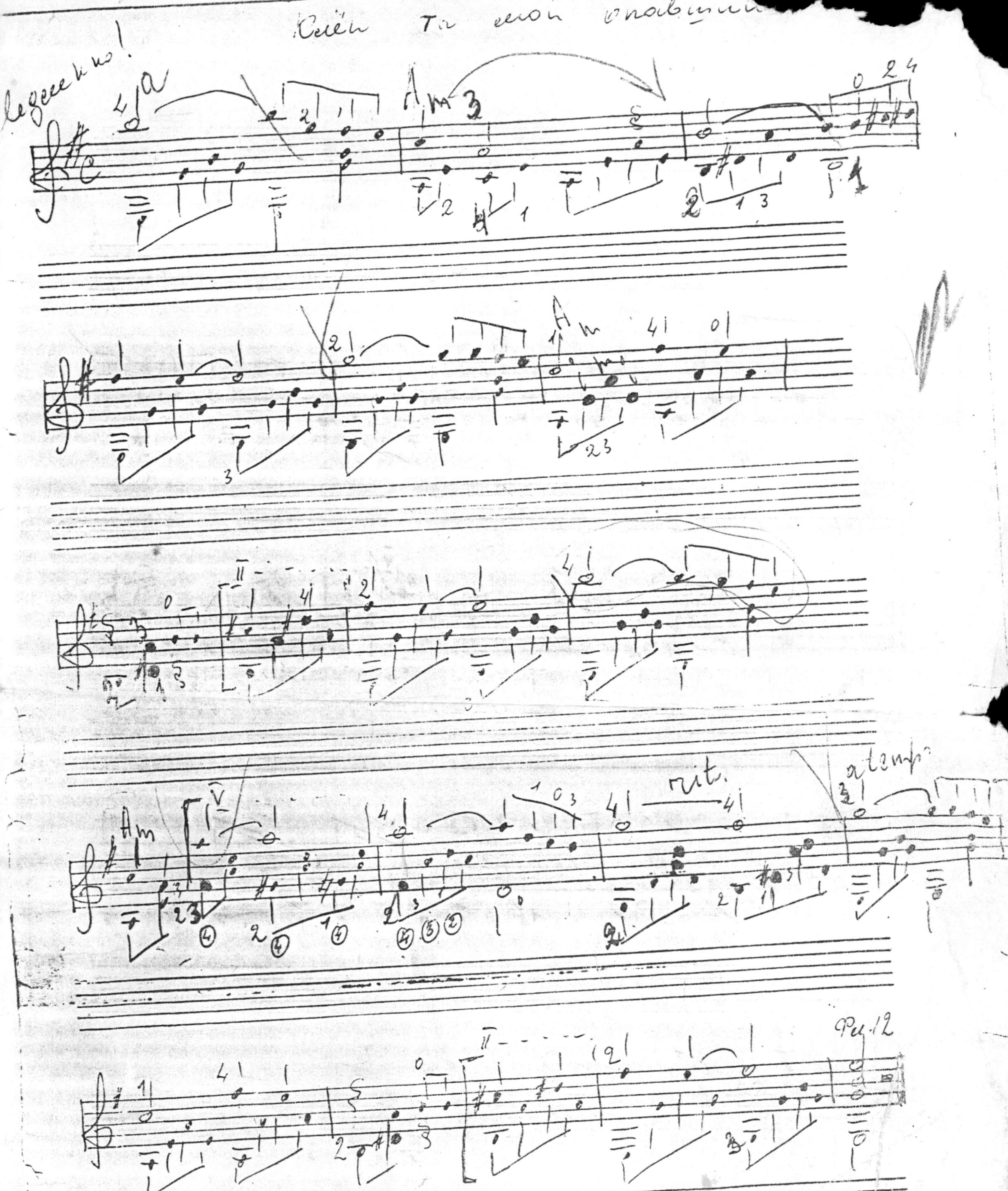
Am
rit.

СТАРИННАЯ ИТАЛЬЯНСКАЯ ПЕСНЯ

Обработка Л. Моццани

Andantino (Не спеша)

14115

Ах ты, душечка

Русская народная песня

Обработка А. Иванова-Крамского

РОНДО

Allegretto

D.C. al Fine